From:

7 Reasons to be Grateful You're the Mother of a

# newborn

*Laura Speidel*

New Leaf Press
*A Division of New Leaf Publishing Group*

# 7 Reasons to be Grateful You're the Mother of a Newborn

First Printing: December 2006

ISBN-13: 978-0-89221-650-5
ISBN-10: 0-89221-650-6
Library of Congress Catalog Number: 2006937326

Cover and Interior Design: LeftCoast Design, Portland, OR 97219
Printed in Italy

For information regarding author interviews, please
contact the publicity department at (870) 438-5288.

Please visit our website for other great titles:
www.newleafpress.net

## table of contents

## Dedicated to. . .

Jamey—A chord of three strands and a lifetime of
happiness. I love you bigger than the sky.

Christian, Landon & Kellen—I can't think of a team I'd
rather play on. I'm honored to share this life with
you. I love you.

Mom and Dad—God blessed me when he placed me in
your care. Thank you for your courage, class, and
abundant love. You are a constant example to me
on this journey.

Joy, Kori, and Rita—You make my life better every day.
Thank you for your faithful friendship.

Dr. Hesla, Dr. Watson, Suzanne, and Linda—You went above
and beyond to make our baby dreams a reality.

Heather—Our friendship is like comfort food for my soul.
Years pass but it's like we never left.

# CHAPTER 1

# Gratefulness

means we get a

do-over day

N o one can prepare you for having a newborn. "It will change your life," they say. "You'll never love anything more," they smile. The nurses gently rolled me out of the hospital and tucked us into our car. The door slammed and we were off. "That's it?" I thought. "This is goodbye? Who cut the umbilical cord when I wasn't looking?"

We'd been home from the hospital 24 hours and I hadn't closed my eyes once. I was beginning to think I would never need mascara, let alone shoes, again. "Fashion" quickly became a bow tied around the waist of my terrycloth robe, accessorized with a nice, clean burp cloth. On a good day I brushed beyond my front teeth. Motherhood had me working day, swing, and graveyard shifts. Every burp, tear, and sneeze was a new line on my resume'. Proudly counting fingers and toes, I struggled to find the "me" in mother. I longed for just one hour without responsibility, yet I craved this new little being.

I allowed two hours to get ready— plenty of time for people who don't have to worry about complete diaper blowouts …

I wanted to hear him breathing, but at the same time I wanted my precious little bundle back where he had come from so I'd know for certain that he was okay, always.

A mother's appetite for complete control coupled with severe sleep deprivation is a dangerous combination. I remember my son's first pediatrician appointment. He was just three days old. As if the transition from womb to home wasn't enough for us, we had to brave the cold December weather for a weight check. I allowed two hours to get ready—plenty of time for people who don't have to worry about complete diaper blowouts, projectile spit-up burps, and pacifier hunts that take you under every couch cushion in the house. No list, no amount of time, no superhuman powers could have prepared me for that day. For a fleeting moment I felt like I couldn't do it. Like I had given birth to a new me—one who would never see another pedicure or spend a warm day driving in a convertible that wasn't "car seat compatible."

I had everything but diapers in the diaper bag.

Then it hit me: God has His hand in every facet of my life, from the packing of the diaper bag to the unpacking of the baggage in my emotional trunk. I quickly saw my purpose in a simple day that wasn't so simple anymore. The morning's events looked less like a debacle and more like an adventure. After all, we'd ventured out into the cold December ice. We'd dodged coughs and sneezes in a petri dish of a waiting room. We were fumbling through our first doctor's appointment together. And when I finally heard them call my baby's first and last name, I stood proudly, knowing we'd arrived. I had everything but diapers in the diaper bag. The car seat straps were too loose and the baby's hat was too tight. But my faith was just right. Ready for anything. Just like God.

# Gratefulness

says a sense of humor is

the best medicine

A person without a sense of humor is like a wagon without springs. It's jolted by every pebble on the road.

Henry Ward Beecher

*Humor Works*

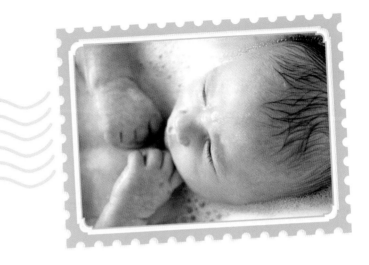

There's something cruel about the sleep deprivation that sets in during the third trimester. The tossing, turning, itching, and aching. You need a hoist to peel yourself from the bed for another trip to the restroom. You lay there, short of breath from turning over, wishing you'd packed a lunch for the walk to the restroom. With a weightlifter's grunt, you use the one, small strand of an abdominal muscle you have left and up you go. It isn't pretty. Your toes are numb, your legs are weak, there's no sense in looking down because you're swollen like a pastry. By the time you get back to bed, it's time to do it again. And now you need a snack.

The season of sacrifice begins. "You look beautiful," they say. "You have that glow!" *That glow* is sweat from a pregnancy hot flash. Somewhere between the second and third trimesters, you lose your voice and your vote when it comes to your changing body.

> Of course there's the classic, "When is your baby due?" that comes a month after you've delivered.

So you surrender—for now. Your ribs become a jungle gym and your bladder a trampoline. The aches and pains of pregnancy are overshadowed by kicks, hiccups, and crib bumpers. A little heartburn becomes a laughing matter and a lot of ice cream becomes routine.

Just when you find the joy and humor in pregnancy, you're left searching for a way to hide your postpartum belly. Nothing fits, you still look five months pregnant, and you have dark circles under your eyes. Of course there's the classic, "When is your baby due?" that comes a month after you've delivered. Or the nursing bra that unsnaps in public, almost taking out your left eye. You're doused by the "fountain of youth" during every diaper change. And there's nothing like a baby toot in the middle of a church service. Though humiliating, they become moments you can snicker about with other moms who are also on this rickety train.

About the time you become comfortable vividly describing diapers in adult conversation, it hits you like a pound of formula. You need to get out. You need to get your laugh back. And you need to do it now.

Suddenly, public diaper tremors are funny. The pile of bills on your desk becomes a great coffee coaster. Four-hour stints of uninterrupted sleep bring reason to smile, and the job is tolerable again. And so we go on mothering our miracles amidst challenge and defeat, while relying on a God who has enough of a funny bone to fine-tune our hearts so we find the sweet humor in the job. Frustrating? Sometimes. Funny? When you look at it in the right light. It's one of the great secrets of motherhood. And the mother who finds it first gets the last laugh.

# CHAPTER 3

# Gratefulness

means we are thankful that

God has a plan

nfertility is a cruel roller coaster. I spent years trying *not* to get pregnant because we weren't ready. We had too much to do—traveling, careers, us. It was as if we thought we could flip the baby switch the moment we were ready.

The day we decided it was time to start a family was invigorating. We figured it would take a month or two but the short wait would make it more exciting.

7 reasons to be grateful you're the mother of a **newborn**

Some "short wait" *that* was. Months went by. I wondered why "it" wasn't happening. This shouldn't be taking so long. What on earth could be wrong?

> I often looked at my husband and wondered if I'd ever see his thick dark hair and long, shiny eyelashes on a child of our own.

We waited. And waited. And waited. We got a puppy. We took a vacation. We redecorated our home. We landscaped. We had our house so organized that the only thing left to buy was one of those fancy garden hose boxes that actually winds the hose for you. The cycle continued and the fear that we would never have a child of our own grew.

I often looked at my husband and wondered if I'd ever see his thick dark hair and long, shiny eyelashes on a child of our own.

Baby showers came and went. We made trips to the hospital to see new babies, leaving empty-handed each time. We didn't want to be the couple in the neighborhood without kids. You know them—the folks who wander the streets each weekend

with mochas and purebred dogs; her hair perfectly styled, his outfit looking like the page of a men's outerwear catalog. Even though they're great together, something—someone—is missing.

*They say if you want to make God laugh, tell him your plan.*

Now we smile at the couple wandering the suburb streets with fancy espresso drinks and well-groomed dogs.

*We were way off course. We* weren't following our plan. People have made millions on products that help women avoid getting pregnant. You don't even have to leave the house to do it (in fact, it's preferable that you don't!). Yet we couldn't seem to make it happen.

*A little hope and a lot of dialing can change everything.*

We began to reach out to infertility clinics, adoption agencies and friends with similar experiences. We quickly realized we weren't off track. The path had simply changed. A little conception turbulence had forced us to take a different route—one that included rigorous testing, quick results, and a miracle conception through fertility treatments.

*The journey was long and lonely but the destination sweet.*

Now *we* smile at the couple wandering the suburb streets with fancy espresso drinks and well-groomed dogs. Why? They are proof of what God will do with *his* plan, in *his* time. Of course, the grass is always greener. A shower, some trendy outerwear, and a double-tall-no-whip-lotta-fancy-stuff-in-a-cup look pretty desirable when you're pushing a baby jogger on three hours of sleep.

# CHAPTER 4

# Gratefulness

means we are thankful

for the people in our lives

I remember learning how to merge onto the freeway with my mom. I could smell the new leather interior as I sat quietly in the passenger seat. I could see her neatly trimmed platinum blonde hair and tapestry purse in my peripheral vision as I stared at the dashboard. I listened very carefully to her instructions on merging—not out of interest, but to show her that I was ready for the fast lane.

"Merging is something that will come naturally," she said. "But you have to be careful—as you become more comfortable, you will look for shortcuts. You'll skip the blinker to save time. You won't allow enough stopping time. You'll forget to check your rearview mirror. Remember, driving is a privilege that deserves our undivided attention. And by the way, anyone who stops on an on-ramp is *asking* to be rear-ended. Now, watch me merge once and then you can try."

"Note to self," I thought.
"Don't stop on the on-ramp."

"Note to self," I thought. "Don't stop on the on-ramp." And we were off! Mom had planned ahead. We were out before the rest of the world was awake, and she'd picked a ramp that seemed a mile long. I could see the accelerator go down beneath her leather-tasseled shoe. She was looking over her shoulder, checking her mirrors and explaining how it was our responsibility to yield. Soon we were doing 35mph. Then 45. Then 50. She flipped on her left blinker as gravity forced my head against the leather seat. I figured she had the wheel— she'd done this a million times before—but how was she missing the red semi-truck that was driving precisely where we would be merging? I dug my fingernails into the leather and asked, "Now what?" As the truck driver blew his horn, her brake pedal went down, we flew forward, and the car came to a screeching halt. The red semi blew by in a cloud of exhaust as we sat there, laughing, completely stopped at the end of the on-ramp. "One more thing," she said, "things don't always go as planned. When that happens, you simply start again."

Motherhood moves at light speed and when you become comfortable, everything changes.

It's one of many lessons I learned from my mom. When all I could think about were earrings, boys and how I was going to get my mom to hand over the keys, our merging moment was settling into the dark corners of my brain. I carried it for years without even knowing it was there. And one day, when nothing was going right with my children, I realized that motherhood is much like merging. You plan for everything, yet you are prepared for nothing. You follow all of the signs and before you know it, you're lost and alone. Just when you're ready to join the mainstream, a big, loud, ugly challenge is in your lane. Motherhood moves at light speed and when you become comfortable, everything changes. You miss exits, meet confrontations and collide with circumstances you'd never expected. Then you pick up the pieces and start again with pride. It began as a silly experience, yet it serves as a reminder that the sweet hearts God places in the driver's seat change our lives forever.

# Gratefulness

means we thank God

for the job

We all have a vision of the ultimate mother. Mine was derived from my mom. She made it look so easy. I had been banking on that vision becoming reality our first week home from the hospital. We were a family now. My husband and I would slip into our new roles and it would be smooth sailing.

I had imagined flaunting my strengths: settling a fussy baby, tidying my perfect nursery, stuffing my post-pregnancy love handles back into my low-rise jeans and heading out on the town with my sleek, black diaper bag. As the days flew by, I waited for that "bounce-back" moment. After all, I was designed for this job. This should be easy.

> As the days flew by, I waited for that "bounce-back" moment. After all, I was designed for this job. This should be easy.

One evening while rocking my son, I realized my expectations of motherhood had been replaced by reality. On that night we had a little talk, my tiny son and I. Not surprisingly, I did most of the talking.

Although he was too young to remember, I know I will never forget.

"I am your mom. I read countless books on sleep training and we broke all of the rules the first week. I planned to nurse for months and I was ready to quit our first day home. I never knew what sleep deprivation could do to a marriage. And when everyone asks how I am adjusting, I smile and get up to warm a bottle.

"The dark circles under my eyes will be a testimony to ear infections, bad dreams and broken curfews. I will invest more time in lunch box notes than most people spend writing wills. I believe signing a check with a dull, red crayon is perfectly acceptable if it happens to be at the top of the diaper bag at the time.

"I've studied faces, photos and figures and I am certain there is none more beautiful than you. Whether that's because you are mine or because you are the benchmark for beauty matters little. I'm in the middle of reading thirteen books about you, and the photos on my nightstand are stacked so high that I'll be scrap booking until I'm 80. I've memorized your length, weight, and head circumference but I have no idea what day it is.

> Someday, I will lay down the duties of motherhood and if I'm lucky, you will call me 'friend.'

"I have the ability to sleep through the freight train snoring next to me but a sigh on your baby monitor wakes

me instantly. My lullabies are out of tune. My nursery rhymes
are incomplete. But my time is free.

"The time will come when you won't want me around.
You'll want me to drop you off before our destination as you

struggle to find your independence. Although it will sting, I'll do my best to respect your space.

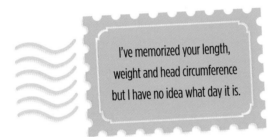

I've memorized your length, weight and head circumference but I have no idea what day it is.

"We'll laugh, cry, dream, and hurt. There will be seasons where I love you though I have nothing left to give, and others where you sustain me. The older you grow, the more our relationship will evolve. Someday, I will lay down the duties of motherhood and if I'm lucky, you will call me 'friend.'

"Mine is the only career that provides a lifetime of on-the-job training. God designed me expressly to do this special work.

My heart has been walking around outside of my body since the day you were born. And I wouldn't have it any other way."

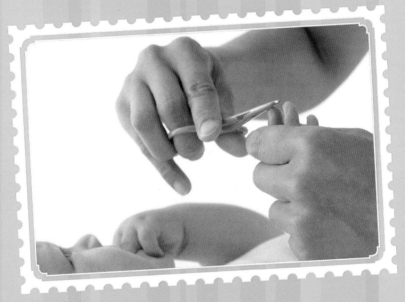

**Gratefulness**

means we thank God

for our strengths

and weaknesses

Sometimes the strength of motherhood

is greater than natural laws.

Barbara Kingsolver

When I met him it was love at first sight. He was anything *but* what I expected. Not blonde and blue-eyed. Not fair skinned. He certainly wasn't a carbon copy of his brother. I loved his dark, shiny hair. His stormy hazel eyes and thick black eyelashes were heaven to look at. I could get used to this—something different—something unique.

The first weeks were a juggling act. Was there enough of my time to go around? Would I ever have time alone with him? His entire life was looking like a hand-me-down.

One evening, while trying to free myself from a baby sling, I looked over and he was in the arms of his brother: a pure and innocent toddler who had nothing to give but time. He was gentle because that was all he knew. As they smiled at each other, I saw a lifetime of friendship. At a time when I was being pulled in many directions, my toddler—the same child who had just jammed three

> My toddler—the same child who had jammed three Cheerios® up his nose moments ago—was picking up the slack.

Cheerios up his nose—was picking up the slack. I instantly recalled a piece of advice I had received while pregnant. "Second babies may not get as much of your time, but they instantly inherit a family with more hearts to love."

It was true—our family was more refined, more established. I've had to let go of many of the expectations I had for him. His shoes are already scuffed. His overalls have patches over the knees. The pages of his books are torn. But his home has been filled to the rooftop with abundant love, all for him. When he cries, his big (or not so big) brother is right there with a pacifier or a hug. He has a playmate for life. And years from now, when parents are anything but cool, he'll have a companion. Sure, there will be fights over dump trucks, diggers, and much bigger things. But they'll always have each other.

Now, my littlest one looks to his big brother for laughs. When he wakes from his nap he scours the room until he finds a bouncing toddler because his tiny life isn't complete without

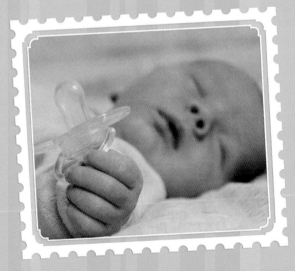

his friend. The parts of his baby heart that are renewed daily by his brother simply couldn't be filled by anyone else—not even me.

God gave me wisdom when he opened my eyes to their interactions that day in my weakness. I was searching for perfection for this baby as though he was my only focus. As I unsuccessfully attempted to balance swaddling and shoe tying, the power of family prevailed. My guilt quickly became contentment as I watched two young and innocent souls, each with unique hearts, meeting each other's needs on a daily basis as only they can.

# CHAPTER 7

# Gratefulness

means we thank God

for the journey

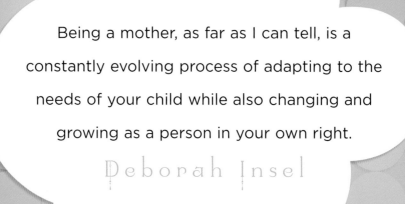

Being a mother, as far as I can tell, is a constantly evolving process of adapting to the needs of your child while also changing and growing as a person in your own right.

Deborah Insel

L ife with baby has not only provided a rapid change
of pace, but also a change of purpose. When it was
all about me, it was all about the next handbag or lip
liner. Whether neckerchiefs were in or out. How I was going
to find the right ankle socks for my trendy slip-on sneakers.
I slept in when I wanted. I ate what I wanted. I even indulged

when I wanted to. Consequences? Well, those were things
like overdue parking meters, early conference calls, and that
burning indentation your jeans leave around your midsection
after too much cheesecake the night before. Life was easy.
But it was lonely.

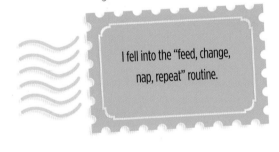

I fell into the "feed, change,
nap, repeat" routine.

When we
brought my son
home from the
hospital I was
prepared for

anything. Batteries were in the swings. Teethers were ready
for teething. I fell into the "feed, change, nap, repeat" routine.
Before I knew it, I was shoving food into

my mouth with one hand, warming a bottle with the other. I wondered if I'd ever find that place again—the place that was mine mentally and physically, the place where I could realign my goals and revisit my dreams. I didn't need to do anything significant in my place as much as I needed a corner all my own.

The house felt crowded. My mind felt like I couldn't cram

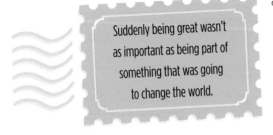

Suddenly being great wasn't as important as being part of something that was going to change the world.

one more thought into it. Diapers, wipes, slings, baby soap— not to mention how I was going to raise this child without *completely* screwing him up. I couldn't see light at the end of the tunnel because I was so focused on the next milestone in our daily schedule.

One day I saw the big picture. This precious little gift was bound for great things and I was fortunate enough to be a part of it. Suddenly, being great wasn't as important as being part of something that was going to change the world. I saw it in his eyes. Big, blue, innocent, powerful eyes. He was going to

grow. Fast! I needed to get busy. What was I going to contribute?
I had so much to teach him. Preschool was only three years
away! I needed to get on waiting lists. What if he didn't know
his colors? Wait! This "motherhood thing" really does require
more than binkies and bottle brushes.

If that wasn't God's call to purpose, I'm not sure what is.
Each day is a balancing act between my responsibilities as a
mother and the dreams I have for myself. Each new stage finds
me peeking around the corner in search of equilibrium and I
have yet to find it. Perhaps it's a journey that won't end until
my kids are grown and gone, at which point I'll have abundant
time to realize my dreams, overshadowed by a deep longing to
simply serve my children.

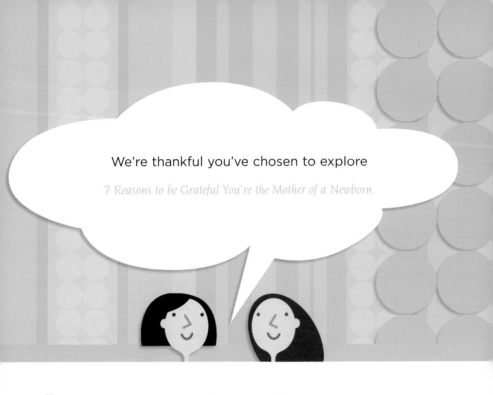

We're thankful you've chosen to explore

*7 Reasons to be Grateful You're the Mother of a Newborn.*

•••••• If these essays have made you recall your own

for-better-or-worse moments, take a few minutes

to write some thoughts to perhaps share with your

child(ren) sometime... like after they have their *own* kids.

## How Many Do-Over Days Can We Have?

Sometimes during a long string of seemingly wasted days, we long for meaning, purpose, and some guarantee this child-rearing gig will turn out positively. Is there a time you can look back on, now from a different perspective, when the dreariness of day-to-day family duties produced a bit of hope after a long, dry spell?

## When Your Sense of Humor is Buried Beneath Your Laundry...

Immediately following 9/11, New York Mayor Rudy Giuliani suggested we needed to find a way to laugh again—while we're still crying. Some might suggest this applies to motherhood as well. Can you recall some times when laughter gave way to tears . . . and tears gave way to laughter?

## What's the Master Plan?

It's been said that life has to be lived forward, but can only be understood backwards. As a mom, what experiences have you had that have shifted your view of your plans versus God's plans? In what areas are you still hoping your plans will win?

As Hillary Clinton noted, it takes a village to raise a child. Who are the members of your tribe, your people? How have they helped you raise your family? In what areas do you feel you *have* to go it alone?

## It's a Tough Job, But Someone's Got to Do It...

Some say parenting is the only job for which we apply without a clue of what we're doing. Do you view parenting as a chore? A job? A gift? How has it been different from what you expected or hoped for?

D o you feel hand-picked by God to parent your specific kids? Does this notion change your view of your own strengths and weaknesses?